The Transitive VAMPIRE

The Transitive VAMPIRE

A Handbook of GRAMMAR
for the Innocent,
the Eager,
and the Doomed

Karen Elizabeth Gordon

SEVERN HOUSE PUBLISHERS

This title first published in Great Britain 1985 by
SEVERN HOUSE PUBLISHERS LTD of
4 Brook Street, London W1Y 1AA
First published in the USA by Times Books 1984

Copyright © 1984 by Karen Elizabeth Gordon

British Library Cataloguing in Publication Data
Gordon, Karen Elizabeth
  The transitive vampire: an adult guide to
  grammar.
  1. English language—Grammar—1950-
  I. Title
  428.2   PE1112

ISBN 0 7278 2080 X
ISBN 0 7278 2073 7 Pbk

Designed by Doris Borowsky

Printed and bound in Great Britain by
Anchor Brendon Ltd, Tiptree, Essex

❀ REMEMBRANCE ❀ OF THINGS TO COME

This book was written in transit, as it and I moved around, and the presence and encouragement of many people contributed to its careening course. I wish to thank Kay Turney, Shirley Young, Les and Camilla Collins, Paul and Sue Gordon, Michael Bruce, Linda Purdy, my editor, Elisabeth Scharlatt, Francois Hébert, Nicole Piché, Carol Dunlop, Julio Cortázar, and Maia Gregory, the sorceress of the apprentice.

Among the others are sentences for Andrei Codrescu, Jean-Jacques Passera, Dorothy Overly, Pat Nolan, David Bromige, Richard Joyce, Luis Tomasello, Stephen Marcus, Silvia Monrós-Stojaković, and Mrazovac Drago Rastislav.

✾ CONTENTS ✾

❦ INTRODUCTION ❦

*Like everything metaphysical the harmony between
thought and reality is to be found in the grammar of
the language.*

Wittgenstein
Zettel, 55

It is not often that circumstances force me to utter more than
one sentence at a time, or, for that matter, one after another—
the usual arrangement of such things. And we are dealing with
usual arrangements here: the form and ordering of words, be
they mumbled, bellowed, or inscribed. Grammar is a *sine qua
non* of language, placing its demons in the light of sense, sentencing them to the plight of prose. Don't take an immediate
and sullen dislike to this book or look askance before you've
even begun. Do not mangle it yet. By allowing yourself to be
misled by the subject you will end up more intimate with the
knowledge that you already possess.

This is a dangerous game I'm playing, smuggling the in-
junctions of grammar into your cognizance through a ménage
of revolving lunatics kidnapped into this book. Their stories
are digressions toward understanding, a pantomime of raucous
intentions in the linguistic labyrinth. By following them
through this rough and twisting terrain you will be beguiled
into compliance with the rules, however confounding those
rules may appear to be. Learning is less a curse than a distrac-

tion. If you nuzzle these pages with abandon, writing will lose its terror and your sentences their disarray. I am not trifling with your emotions, nor flapping an antic mirage in your face. Whether you dawdle or maraud your way through these pages, you will return to them repeatedly to slake your thirst. The impending savvy is yours for the taking. You don't even have to ask.

Before I leave you in the embrace of the transitive vampire, I should introduce him to you, for he too went through the dubious process of education and came out none the worse for wear. He was not always a vampire. He can recall the bitter-sweet pleasure of a morsel of marzipan dissolving on his tongue and earlier memories of the vanished bliss of his mother's breast. He was a child of immense generosity and voracious intellect. By the age of ten he had read all of Tolstoy and Pushkin and *The Torments of Timofey*, a neglected Slavic epic that greatly affected his sensibility and filled his young mind with dread. He knew suffering from inside out, abjection like the back of his hand, which was slender and silken and thrilling to all who were touched by him.

When his manhood set in, our hero set out from home to seek his fortune, or at least his way. The mountains of his mother country were monstrously metaphysical. Words reposed in stones, and it was here, high above the cradle of his childhood, that his nature and purpose revealed themselves, not far from the howling wolves. No one knows quite how it happened, but he came back decidedly changed, transfixed through some secret effect. He had become one of night's creatures, with a grammar he had received from the great and jagged unknown. Treading carefully among the broken rules, he returned to set things straight. It was a noble undertaking, and it was noted in his epitaph, although he is immortal, like language itself, and still prowling around.

The Transitive
VAMPIRE

✺ SENTENCES ✺
and What We Mean by Them

This is a book of sentences: sentences about sentences, and sentences sentencing themselves. If you want to write, and I hope you do, the sentence is your point of departure. Part of the art of creating a sentence is knowing the substance and elements of which it is composed. We all know, or let us assume, that sentences are made of words. But words come in various guises, whatever they are intended to hide or reveal, and so we must begin with them—seeing just what they think they are, as grammarians have defined them, and bringing them together into the realm of sense.

A sentence is a group or string or alignment of words expressing a complete thought. You can have your incomplete thoughts as well, but if you want to get a sense of completion out of them, you'll have to follow the rules. To be a sentence, and thereby constitute an independent item of expression with as much integrity as you wish to dress it in, a succession of words must have a subject and a predicate. These are the two essential parts of a sentence.

The Subject

The subject is that part of the sentence about which something is divulged; it is what the sentence is talking about.

> *The girl* is squatting under the bridge.
> *The girl squatting under the bridge* is a debutante.
> *The mutant* chuckled.
> *The door* opened.
> *The contraption* shut.
> *He* was caught.
> How wicked *to behold you*.
> *There* were *fifty-five lusterless vampires* dismantling the schloss.
> *His huge, calm, intelligent hands* wrestled with her confusion of lace.
> How slipshod *their courtship* was.
> *The werewolf* had a toothache.
> *The afflicted fang* caused him to wince pathetically as he stifled his sobs in his sleeve.
> *The persona non grata* was rebuked.
> *The door* slammed in his flabbergasted face.

The *italicized* words in the above sentences form the complete subject. The simple subject, a noun or pronoun, is the essence lurking at its center, without which the complete subject would be nothing at all. In the sentences below, only the simple subjects are italicized:

> The *painting* leered.
> The *prince* demurred.
> The *innuendo* flying over her head was a come-on.

The persona non grata was rebuked.

A *morsel* of humility would help.
The spritely *lummox* faltered.

The Predicate

The predicate is the other necessary part of the sentence, the part that has something to say about the subject, that states its predicament.

The debutante *is squatting under the bridge.*
The werewolf *had a toothache.*
The door *slammed in his flabbergasted face.*
The contraption *shut.*

The complete predicate of a sentence consists of all the words that divulge something about the subject. Like the complete subject, the complete predicate has an essence, a fundamental reality, called the simple predicate, or verb.

The debutante *is squatting* under the bridge.
The werewolf *had* a toothache.
The door *slammed* in his flabbergasted face.

Compounds

Both simple subjects and simple predicates can be compound, which means that more than one thing is going on, or is being gone on about.

A compound subject contains two or more subjects, joined by *and, or,* or *nor,* which share the same verb, are doing the same thing, are sharing the same predicament.

> A *debutante* and *a troll* are squatting under the
> bridge.
> *The werewolf* or *his wife* wreaked havoc in the
> pantry.
> *The innuendo* and *its consequences* missed their
> mark completely.

A compound predicate, or compound verb, is the happy
issue of two or more verbs that are joined by *and, or,* or
nor and that belong to the same subject.

> The recluse *groveled* before the mannequin and
> *kissed* the hem of her slip.
> She *wriggled* in acknowledgment or *writhed* in
> uncalled-for shame.
> The debutante *squatted* and *pondered* her
> meaningless life.
> The werewolf *howled* piteously and *sought*
> comfort in the lap of his wife.
> His huge, calm, intelligent hands *swerved*
> through the preliminaries and *wrestled* with
> her confusion of lace.
> It neither *soothed* the unrecorded regrets nor
> *averted* the impending doom.

I fancy dames with broad shoulders.

❧ WORDS ❧
and What Kinds of Words They Are

Just to keep things straight, and to straighten you out, words are categorized, in accordance with their behavior, into eight parts of speech: nouns, pronouns, verbs, adjectives, adverbs, prepositions, conjunctions, and interjections. Many words can be used as several different parts of speech. The part of speech a word is classified as in a given instance is revealed by how it is used:

VERB:

> I *fancy* dames with broad shoulders.

ADJECTIVE:

> Her *fancy* dress showed them off to great advantage.

NOUN:

> I therefore took a *fancy* to her.

VERB:

> The vampire began to *powder* his nose.

NOUN:

> The *powder* made him sneeze all over the mirror,
> in which he could not see himself anyway.

NOUN:

> The *bulge* in his jacket made him look pregnant.

VERB:

> He used to *bulge* all over.

NOUN:

> His *pants* are bulging, too.

VERB:

> She *pants* at the sight of him.

NOUN:

> The *throbbing* made her reel and fall.

VERB:

> He was *throbbing* with pleasure at this sight.

Nouns

A noun is a word that names a person, place, thing, or abstraction. Abstractions may include emotions, ideas, qualities, notions, wishes, passions, attributes, etc.

PERSON:

> ballerina, curator, Desdemona, midwife, girl,
> boy, coward, alchemist, tenor, zoologist,
> eavesdropper, impresario, editor, ruffian,

zealot, somnambulist, cellist, pimp, nomad,
hit-man, philosopher, glutton, Harpo Marx,
dilettante, sadist, waitress, Peter Lorre,
Mozart, necromancer, starlet

PLACE:

Aix-en-Provence, Alabama, Sevastopol, Kyoto,
Rio de Janeiro, Alsace-Lorraine, Lithuania,
Chicago, Omsk, Mars

THING:

cigar, pocket, mirror, bubble, gonad,
trombone, marzipan, stalactite, toothpick,
taco, shadow, scum, ivory, clock, omphalos,
snow, cup, swamp, bonbon, piroshki,
mosquito, ribbon, hand, haunch

ABSTRACTION:

finesse, ubiquity, afterlife, yelp, monogamy,
moan, solitude, monad, fashion, horror,
Cubism, archangel, aroma, silence, siesta,
malapropism, ethos, pride, cataclysm,
revenge

Compound nouns are nouns made up of more than one
word:

box office, soap opera, Nova Scotia, rite of
passage, miracle play, small talk, looking
glass, cream puff, eye shadow, black hole

Pronouns

A pronoun also names, by taking the place of a noun. The

noun for which the pronoun is stepping in is called its antecedent.

> *The chap with the long face* is buying *his* insurance policy.
> *The guys at the gym* were snapping *their* towels.
> *The girls in the corner* are waiting to do *their* number.
> There was *a lull in the conversation. It* was embarrassing.
> What is the name of *that surly bloke*? I'm dying to meet *him*.

The pronoun stands for the other words accompanying the noun as well as the noun itself. Thus, *his* replaces all of *the chap with the long face; him* replaces not only the bloke but his surliness, too.

Adjectives

An adjective describes, or limits, a noun or pronoun.

Descriptive adjectives state what kind of person, place, or thing a noun is:

> *spitting* image, *bashful* poltergeist, *portable* landscape, *sugar-coated* speech, *injured* appendage, *wrong* track

Limiting adjectives give some idea of the quantity or identity of the noun being discussed. Limiting adjectives are of several sorts.

POSSESSIVE ADJECTIVES:

> *my* shyness, *his* standoffishness, *her* apprehension,

The girls in the corner are waiting to do their number.

our shame, *their* greed, *your* delusions

which nodule? *whose* xenophobia? *what* quirk?

DEMONSTRATIVE ADJECTIVES:

this contretemps, *those* rhapsodies, *that* samovar, *these* mishaps

ARTICLES:

an Anglophile, *the* promontory, *a* zipper

NUMERICAL ADJECTIVES:

one grin, *two* guffaws, *second* thought, *third* snort

Usually placed directly before the noun it is describing as in the above sentences, an adjective can also come after the predicate, connected to the noun by a linking verb, such as *be* or *seems*.

Dawn kissed the horizon with its *fresh, hot* lips.
The lips of dawn were *fresh* and *hot*.

His *bleary* eyes stared back at him.
His eyes seemed *bleary* as they stared back at him.

Verbs

A verb is a word or group of words asserting something about the subject of the sentence. The assertion may describe an action or it may express identity or state of being.

Her fiancé is a somnambulist.

ACTION:

> The waif *whimpered*.
> The onlooker *ogled*.
> The aristocrat *undulated*.
> The bistro *burned*.

STATE OF BEING:

> Her fiancé *is* a somnambulist.
> His dreams *are* mobile.

Some verbs contain one or more auxiliary or helping verbs:

> The miracle *had been* invoked.
> The fracas *will have* hastened the propinquity
>   they longed to feel.
> We *have been* scrounging.

Adverbs

An adverb modifies a verb. It may also modify an adjective or another adverb, thus consorting with its own kind.

> She guffawed *helplessly*.
> She was *rather* helpless.
> She guffawed *rather* helplessly.
>
> He gaped *primly*.
> He was *very* prim.
> He gaped *very* primly.
>
> She beckoned *crassly*.
> She was *exceedingly* crass.
> She beckoned *exceedingly* crassly.

He groped *hesitantly*.
He was *very* hesitant.
He groped *very* hesitantly.

Adverbs tell when, how, where, and to what extent an action is done or a state of being exists:

TIME:

He came *immediately*.

MANNER:

We snuffled *apologetically*.

PLACE:

I must loiter *here*.

DEGREE:

She was *quite* inconsolable.
He was *most* invincible.
I was *very* miserable.
He was *quite* affable.
They were *very* jolly.

Prepositions

Prepositions indicate the relation of a noun or pronoun to some other word in the sentence. A prepositional phrase is made up of the preposition, the noun or pronoun that is its object, and the modifiers of the object.

He slapped her *on* the scapula.
They toyed *with* the idea amorously.

I was very miserable.

> Lisa shakily stood her ground *with* an
>   obstreperous opposition *of* her puny will.
> We chatted unctuously *into* our bowls *of* soup.
> They waddled *down* the trail *to* the ruins.

Some of the more popular prepositions in our language include:

> above, across, after, along, among, around, at,
>   before, behind, below, beside, besides,
>   between, beyond, but, by, down, during, for,
>   from, in, inside, into, near, of, off, on,
>   outside, over, past, since, through, till, to,
>   toward, towards, under, until, upon, with,
>   within, without

Compound prepositions, or prepositions made of more than one word, also enjoy being used:

> apart from, as for, as well as, aside from,
>   because of, by means of, contrary to, for the
>   sake of, in back of, in case of, in front of, in
>   place of, in spite of, inside of, instead of, out
>   of, together with, up at, up to, with regard
>   to

Conjunctions

Conjunctions are words that join words, phrases, or clauses, just as the word *or* in this sentence links the words *phrases* and *clauses*. Conjunctions are humble and quite useful; you might barely notice them most of the time, but if a conjunction were removed or used out of context, an awkward gap would be felt. In addition to coordinate conjunctions and subordinate conjunctions, there are conjunctive adverbs that act in a connective way.

Coordinate conjunctions join words, phrases, and clauses of equal importance in the same sentence. The most common coordinate conjunctions are *and, but, or, neither, nor, for, whereas,* and *yet.*

> The robot *and* the dentist tangoed beneath the stars.
> They used to meet in the parking lot *or* at a nearby bar.
> They often danced in public, *but* no one seemed to mind.
> *Neither* his existence *nor* his vacuity betrayed his true intent.
> Her antic *yet* coercive repartee confuted his dismay.

Conjunctive adverbs are adverbs that join independent clauses, which may also be whole sentences. They include *accordingly, afterwards, also, besides, consequently, earlier, furthermore, hence, however, later, moreover, nevertheless, otherwise, still, then, therefore,* and *thus.*

> They don't have me down as a bad person yet; *however,* it could happen at any time.

> There is always room for improvement; *moreover,* in this case that's all the room there is.

> She's off in the gazebo having a little crise de nerfs. *Nevertheless,* her eyes will be dry for the big shebang tonight.

If Lucifer confesses, we'll let the rest of you go.

Subordinate conjunctions are how you may get into a dependent clause—one functioning, for example, as an adjective or adverb. If a sentence begins with a dependent clause (as this one does), the subordinate conjunction (in this case, *if*) comes first, so that it can state the condition or circumstance modifying the independent clause. Otherwise, a subordinate conjunction may come between the parts of the sentence it connects.*

> *If* Lucifer confesses, we'll let the rest of you go.
> *After* they removed the leeches, she showed him to the door.
> *If* God exists, why would he want to hang around?
> They dropped the subject *before* it got too hot.
> I took an instant liking to him *even though* his hands were covered with fur.
> *If* I die first, will you tuck me into my casket?

Here there is something I feel I ought to warn you about. Since a subordinate conjunction at the beginning of a clause renders it incapable of standing alone (as the word *since* does this one), whereas without the conjunction it could stand alone perfectly well, you must watch out for the ever-lurking potential of creating sentence fragments (see page 107) by failing to connect the dependent clause thus established with an accompanying independent clause.

> CORRECT: Well, don't get into a swelter about it, since jeopardy was the inevitable upshot of this stupid farce.

*Other dependent clauses act like nouns, in which capacity they do not concern us here.

Very well, I'll slick your hair down myself.

FRAGMENT: Well, don't get into a swelter
            about it. Since jeopardy was the
            inevitable upshot of this stupid
            farce.

Subordinate conjunctions include *until, since, if, because, after, before, although, that, as if, so that, though, unless, while, when, where, even though,* and *in order that*. Relative pronouns—*who, which, that, whom, whose, what, how*—also function as subordinate conjunctions.

> The behemoth *that* trundled into view was
>   covered with tattoos.
> The interloper, *whom* we had to suppress, was
>   given a ticket to Tangier.
> The thingamabob *which* I sorely need is still
>   evading my grasp.

Interjections

An interjection is a word or collection of words that expresses feeling. An outcast, set apart from the other seven parts of speech, the interjection has little grammatical connection with its neighboring words or sentences. Since it is strong, or emphatic, however, it doesn't really care.

> *Well,* why aren't you on the prowl?
> *Very well,* I'll slick your hair down myself.
> *Oh my!* How lithe you've grown!
> *Dear me,* what cherubic chops you have!
> *Goodness!* What a wallop you pack!
> *Wow!* What unattainable bliss we've nearly
>   achieved!
> *My god!* I must remember your name!

❧ NOUNS ❧

As you already know by now, nouns are names of people, places, things, or abstractions. There are more ways for you to know nouns, though, because they are further classified: once a word is identified as a noun, it can be labeled as one kind or another and used in several different ways.

Common nouns are nouns that utter the name of one or more members of a large class of things:

> rabbit, door, gin, moose, face, limousine, movie, girl, button, tattoo, cookie, lake, silhouette, tulip, storm, wave, trinket, cuff, blues

Proper nouns name a specific person, place, or thing:

> Dionysius, Bela Lugosi, Samuel Beckett, Malta, Egyptology, Big Sur, Gertrude Stein, East 72nd Street, Ubu Roi, The Hound of the Baskervilles, Vivaldi, Austria, London, Oscar Wilde, Transylvania, Guillaume depuis le

Rapprochement, Tiresias, Monty Python,
Mother Goose

Collective nouns are nouns that give names to groups of
things or people:

> squad, flock, herd, gang, orchestra, mob,
> plethora, crowd, horde, audience, harem,
> coterie, gaggle, cluster, caboodle, swarm,
> throng, coven, bevy, galaxy, tribe, suite,
> troupe, bundle

Concrete nouns name an object that is perceivable by the
senses:

> flask, hut, goose, bog, blood, tutu, spoon,
> glove, phone, cream, rose, pipe, calliope,
> moon, harpsichord, thigh, brooch

Abstract nouns name a quality or idea:

> solace, havoc, mood, trouble, hunch, shame,
> fatigue, dismay, miasma, ardor, casuistry,
> pathos, discretion, mourning, luxury, ethics,
> antithesis, paradox, flummery, time

Classifications have a way of breeding confusion as well as
creating order. Collective, concrete, and abstract nouns
are subclasses of common nouns. I hope you understand.

A noun can be used in any of the following ways: as the
subject of a sentence, as a complement of a verb, as an
object of a preposition, as an appositive, and in direct
address.

rabbit

Subject of a Sentence

The subject tells who or what did it, does it, or will do it or reveals who or what is being talked about in the sentence. It is generally placed before the verb. (Later on, you will see how a verb can precede its noun.)

> *Snow* fell.
> *Felix* fumbled.
> *Lizzy* fluttered her eyelashes.
> *Lucy and Ludwig* plighted their troth.
> The *shiksa* shivered.
> The *vampire* snoozed.

Complement of a Verb

When you find or place in the predicate of a sentence a word that completes the meaning of the verb, that word is the complement of the verb. Complements are either direct objects, indirect objects, or subjective or objective complements.

A direct object answers the question *what?* or *whom?* after the verb:

> I scratched the *knee.*
> He chastened *Daisy.*
> Let's just split the *difference.*

The direct object may also be a pronoun:

> I scratched *it.*
> He chastened *her.*
> Let's just split *it.*

An indirect object tells *to* or *for whom* or *what* the action of the verb, however welcome or unwanted, is committed:

> I gave the *gadfly* a piece of my mind.
> I sent *Satchmo* a billet-doux.
> The mannequin gave the *baby vampire* her phone number and returned to her window alone.

A pronoun can also be used as an indirect object:

> I gave *her* a piece of my mind.
> I sent *him* a billet-doux.

A subjective complement comes hot on the heels of a linking verb to explain or identify the subject. If the subjective complement is a noun, it is called a "predicate noun":

> A tingle is a *pleasure.*
> A stepfather is a *faux pas.*
> That fellow traveler is her *bedfellow.*
> Thinking is not her *forte.*
> Your rapture is my *anguish.*
> This harangue is my *relief.*

Pronouns and adjectives can also operate as subjective complements, if you care to give them the chance:

PREDICATE ADJECTIVE:

> That conjuror is *droll.*

PREDICATE PRONOUN:

> I am positive the culprit is *I.*

Subjective complements can follow only these groups of linking verbs: forms of *to be (am, are, is, was, were, been, will be);* verbs of the senses *(look, hear, taste, smell, sound);*

Hey, girlie, drag your carcass over here!

and verbs like *appear, seem, become, grow, prove, remain.*

An objective complement follows and is related to the direct object.

> The prince appointed Gullible *ambassador.*

An objective complement may also be an adjective.

> These furtive tidings made Gwendolyn *gruff.*

Object of a Preposition

This is how a noun looks as the object of a preposition:

> That loaded dotard lives in *squalor.*
> The pendulum swung over the *pit.*
> Tuck yourself in between *Mog and me.*
> You're barking up the wrong *tree.*

Appositive

An appositive further identifies another noun.

> Their caper, an extravagant *interlude,* ended in
> an exhausted embrace.
> The famous courtesan, *Mog Cinders,* was an
> accomplished lepidopterist, too.

Direct Address

In direct address, a noun names the person (or the dog) being spoken to.

Dafne, fetch my spats.

Fido, snatch her purse.

"Well all right, *darling*," she said in a tired
whimper, ambushing the look he gave her
with an affectionate pinch on the cheek.

Hey, *girlie*, drag your carcass over here!

❦ VERBS ❦

The verb is the heartthrob of a sentence. Without a verb, a group of words can never hope to be anything more than a fragment, a hopelessly incomplete sentence, a eunuch or dummy of a grammatical expression. No verb can parade around without a subject, which can be stated openly or simply implied. Even if a sentence is only one word long, as in a command such as *Scram!*, the subject is understood to be *you;* here the verb holds the whole thing together, carrying the burden of the meaning all the way through to the exclamation point and into the reader's head. A verb's purpose in life is to assert, avow, state, imply, insinuate, affirm something about its subject.

> The princess *panhandled.*
> The yak *yearned.*
> The mime *muttered.*
> *Scram!*
> Don't *sashay* out of here without me.
> *Lay* off the mozzarella.

Verbs have met with the same fate that has befallen

nouns: they have been classified! And it is your fate to know, for you are about to learn, what these classifications are. The presence or absence of complements determines the kind of verb a verb is—unless it is an auxiliary verb, which pays less attention to such things. A complement completes a predication, making the predicament whole.

Intransitive verbs are verbs capable of expressing themselves without requiring a complement to complete their meaning.

> The god *thundered*.
> Havelock *blushed*.
> Sophie *sulked* by the spittoon.
> Nemo *slouched* past the fountain.

(In the last two examples, *by the spittoon* and *past the fountain* are adverbial prepositional phrases, not complements.)

Transitive verbs are those that *cannot* complete their meaning without the help of a direct object. The verb is something that someone does to something or someone else.

> We *bounced* the *idea* around the saloon.
> He *yanked her* out of her tedium.
> She *missed* the midnight *train*.

Transitive verbs sometimes take indirect as well as direct objects.

> He *sent* his *fiancée* a *crystal ball*.

(The direct object is *crystal ball;* the indirect object is *fiancée*.)

I am willing and I'll be ready in a while.

These classifications of verbs vary from one sentence to another, depending on how the verb is used. A few verbs (such as *ignore)* are transitive only; others are willing to be entirely intransitive. The labels *v.t.* and *v.i.* used in dictionaries tell you whether a particular meaning of a verb demands an object to complete it.

Linking—or, to put it more explicitly, copulative—verbs link a subject with a subjective complement that describes or explains it. Go back to the note on subjective complements (page 29) if you want to know what these verbs are. Here I will simply allow you to catch them in the act of copulating:

> I *am* willing and I'*ll be* ready in a while.
> She *sounded* eager, but he couldn't be sure.
> They *became* restless and so they went to bed.
> He *is* my solace although he *is* also my pain.
> Trinculo *became* her confidant as the slivovitz
>   disappeared.

Auxiliary verbs are also known as "helping verbs," and they are helpful indeed. To form certain tenses and to express various shades of meaning, one or more special verb forms may be summoned into a sentence to combine with the main verb. These are auxiliary, or helping, verbs. The conjunction of the auxiliary and the verb results in a verb phrase.

> I *may have* done a few things that weren't
>   cricket, but on the whole I *have*n't been all
>   that much out of line.
> He *was* wolfing down his sandwich as his paw
>   fumbled with her knee.

Did you get a cashmere sweater? No, I got a
cashmere life.

A man on the telephone *was* shrieking
"Mommy! Mommy!" so I delicately averted
my face.

She *used to* get loaded every night.

I *might* be able to help you, if you can pick this
lock for me.

Sometimes one or more words may come between the
auxiliary and the main verb. This happens more often
than you may imagine.

Djuna *had* eventually *capitulated*, in response to
our impassioned pleas.

Have any of you *seen* my muff?

Hadn't she *broken* the laws of chance once too
often for such an ingenuous adventuress?

This is the hand to kiss.

❋ VERBALS ❋

Verbals are derived from verbs, but they are *not* verbs because they do not assert anything. Here in their own admirable efforts in the following sentences, you will see just how different they are. Like verbs, verbals may be modified and may require complements to express their meaning. Infinitives, participles, and gerunds are all verbals, each with its own purpose in your prose.

Infinitives

The infinitive is what comes of combining *to* with a verb; it can be used as a noun, an adjective, or an adverb.

INFINITIVES AS NOUNS:

> *To ensnare* is human; *to live,* divine. (subject)
> Sylvie loves *to split* infinitives. (direct object)
> Sylvie wants nothing except *to split* infinitives.
>   (object of preposition)

INFINITIVES AS ADJECTIVES:

> This is the hand *to kiss*. (modifies *hand*)
> These are the pearls *to string*. (modifies *pearls*)
> Those were the blessings *to count*. (modifies *blessings*)
> These are the realities *to lament*. (modifies *realities*)
> Where are the days *to come?* (modifies *days*)
> Such is the will *to live*. (modifies *will*)

INFINITIVES AS ADVERBS:

> Osbert was difficult *to lose*. (modifies *difficult*)
> We opened the door *to eject* him. (modifies *opened*)
> He returned *to plague* us. (modifies *returned*)

Participles

Verbals in the form of a participle are used only as adjectives, but there are still lots of interesting things you can do with them.

Present participles end in *-ing:*

> *Horsing* around satyrically, he leaped into her lap.
> *Scratching* himself coquettishly, he quite won her heart.
> *Smiling* to herself, she wondered what else he could do.
> *Sidling* up to his mother, he asked her for a loan.
> *Begrudging* her son his foibles, she whipped out a wad.

Clambering back to his girl, he proposed a night
    on the town.

Snarling, she jumped for joy.

Rubbing his knees together, he outlined their
    itinerary of dives.

Past participles end in *-d, -ed, -n, -en,* or *-t* (however,
some verbs become past participles through internal
vowel changes, as in *wrung* or *sung*):

Flabbergasted, she acquiesced to his invitation.

Astonished, he pumped her arm.

Exhausted, she begged him to stop.

Overwhelmed, she slouched to the ground.

Puzzled, he tickled her ear.

Undaunted, she continued to swoon.

Embarrassed, he took to his heels.

Unstrung, she recovered her cool.

Gerunds

A gerund is the *-ing* form of a verb; it is there for you to
use as a noun.

Gerunds as Subjects:

Killing time takes practice.

Imploring is humiliating.

Lisping is seductive.

Bumping and *grinding* are among her many
    fascinating tricks.

(Notice that *bumping* and *grinding* as used here are
gerunds, while *fascinating* is an adjective.)

GERUNDS AS DIRECT OBJECTS:

> She enjoys *taunting*.
> He craves *flogging*.

GERUNDS AS SUBJECTIVE COMPLEMENTS:

> Her fear is *losing* control.
> His desire is *gaining* ground.
> Their nightmare is *reaching* limits.

GERUNDS AS OBJECTS OF PREPOSITIONS:

> In *waxing* and *waning,* the moon reflects the
> ways of man.
> By *being* so pregnant with meaning, her
> announcement went over like a lead balloon.
> Through *sporting* a cudgel, the Neanderthal
> made a rude but necessary start.
> By *dunking* her crumpet in the marmalade,
> Melissa committed a midafternoon faux pas.
> In *finding* the chink in his armor, she found
> herself shown to the door.
> By *confessing* her culpabilities, she cleared the
> way for more.

The same *-ing* word (*yelping* and *cringing,* to take two instances) may behave either as a gerund or as a present participle, depending on how it is used. If you use it as a noun, it is a gerund; if you use it as an adjective, it is a participle.

> *Yelping* can be a call for help or a cry of joy.
> *Yelping* loudly, she waited for her prince to
> appear.
>
> *Cringing* is a form of self-defense.
> *Cringing* politely, he ultimately got his way.

*By confessing her culpabilities, she cleared
the way for more.*

▓ MORE ON VERBS ▓

After a few more cautionary words about the handling of
verbs, about to be unleashed, we'll stray into the beguil-
ing realm of modifiers—adjectives and adverbs—which
can alter your meaning drastically.

Tense

If you're going to use a verb, use it in the tense you mean!

PRESENT TENSE:

> I *mope* alone. She *mopes* with others.
> Meteors *rove* the heavens.

PAST TENSE:

> She *moped* in the bistro. I *moped* in my boudoir.

FUTURE TENSE:

> She *will mope* tomorrow when the impulse seizes
> her.

I had moped for five days before
I would touch my gruel.

PRESENT PERFECT TENSE:

> I *have moped* quite enough already for one woebegone and redundant week.

PAST PERFECT TENSE:

> I *had moped* for five days before I would touch my gruel.

FUTURE PERFECT TENSE:

> By the time the Ides of March arrives I *will have moped* for two weeks straight.

Do not needlessly or stupidly shift tense.

WRONG,
STUPID: He *slapped* her on the scapula and *asks* her to grapple with him.

RIGHT: He *slapped* her on the scapula and *asked* her to grapple with him.

WRONG,
STUPID: She *gilded* the lily and *throws* in the towel.

RIGHT: She *gilded* the lily and *threw* in the towel.

Number

Think of the subject of the sentence, the noun or pronoun, and use a verb that matches, or agrees with, it in number. The singular form of the verb is used when the subject refers to only one person or thing; the plural is used when more than one person or thing is referred to.

SINGULAR:

> Dafne *seems* jumpy.
> Solace *soothes* the pain.
> The mutant *sings* the blues.
> There *is* some hanky-panky going on.
> There *is* a midriff beneath his paw.

PLURAL:

> The mutant*s* *sing* the blues.
> The curmudgeon*s* *have* calmed down.
> The quadruped*s* *are* trampling her taffeta gown.
> There *are* unbeaten path*s* she longs to prowl.

Voice

Take it easy on the passive voice. It's too tired to be overused.

ACTIVE:

> The grandee *bullied* the bum.

PASSIVE:

> The bum *was bullied* by the grandee.

ACTIVE:

> The nymphs *dished* it out.

PASSIVE:

> It *was dished* out by the nymphs.

When the person who did it or does it (whatever it is or was) is unknown or unimportant to the sense of the sentence, you may avail yourself of the passive voice:

> The faux pas *was ignored* for several days.
> Her crimes *have been absolved*.
> The grub *was* grudgingly *passed* around.
> The roadhouse *was ransacked* in the middle of the moonless night.

❦ ADJECTIVES ❦
AND ADVERBS

If you can't tell the difference between an adjective and an adverb, you are in for some rough times. Look at the word, sizing up how it is being used or is about to be used by you. Both the function and the form of the word will offer clues to the curious and attentive mind (*curious* and *attentive* here are adjectives because they modify the noun *mind*).

Adjectives describe, or limit, nouns and pronouns:

> an *honest* charlatan, an *undaunted* supplicant, an *adorable* crank, a *redundant* repertoire, a *touchy* subject, a *shoddy* gag, a *supple* limb, a *red* studio, a *sulky* mood

Adverbs describe or limit verbs, sentences, adjectives, or other adverbs:

> The somnambulist stumbled *elegantly*.
> The somnambulist was *very* elegant.
> He stumbled *very* elegantly.

> We roughed it *begrudgingly*.
> We were *awfully* begrudging.
> We roughed it *awfully* begrudgingly.

> The ghoul foraged *hungrily*.
> He was *certainly* hungry!
> The ghoul *certainly* did forage hungrily.

> They soft-pedalled the subject *ceremoniously*.
> They were *rabidly* ceremonious.
> They *rabidly* imposed their ceremonies.

> The orchestra played *mercilessly*.
> We waltzed *Lisztlessly*.

> *Curiously*, the borzoi eschewed the bone.

> *Unexpectedly*, the aggrieving announcement arrived.

Even though many adverbs end in *-ly,* the presence of these two provocative letters at the end of a word is not necessarily a signal that you are staring at an adverb. Pay attention to what the word describes, as well as to how it appears.

> The beauty contest was a toss-up between the *comely* contessa and the *lovely* lamia.
> Those who are meek shall inherit the earth; the *ugly* ones shall have their cake and munch on it, too.

Adverbs, not adjectives, are used to modify verbs, sentences, adjectives, and adverbs.

ADVERBS MODIFYING VERBS:

> He advanced *timorously*. She quivered *enticingly*.

We roughed it begrudgingly.

He grimaced *piously*. She tingled *ambivalently*.
He laughed *remorselessly*. She yammered
rhapsodically.
They plummeted *gleefully*.

WRONG: She sure cut that Gordian knot!

RIGHT: She *surely* cut that Gordian knot!

WRONG: She was put sound in her place.

RIGHT: She was put *soundly* in her place.

WRONG: The orchestra coughed concordant.

RIGHT: The orchestra coughed *concordantly*.

WRONG: The conductor rapped indignant.

RIGHT: The conductor rapped *indignantly*.

WRONG: The Cronopio danced Catalan.

RIGHT: The Cronopio danced *Catalanly*.

ADVERBS MODIFYING SENTENCES:

WRONG: Inexplicable, the muddle was
          familiar enough.

RIGHT: *Inexplicably*, the muddle was familiar
          enough.

WRONG: Imperceptible, the room had ceased to roar.

RIGHT: *Imperceptibly*, the room had ceased to roar.

ADVERBS MODIFYING ADJECTIVES:

WRONG: I was wretched sore.

RIGHT: I was *wretchedly* sore.

WRONG: She was a gaudy clothed cutie.

RIGHT: She was a *gaudily* clothed cutie.

WRONG: He was a dapper dressed vampire.

RIGHT: He was a *dapperly* dressed vampire.

ADVERBS MODIFYING ADVERBS:

WRONG: He bellowed unmerciful loudly.

RIGHT: He bellowed *unmercifully* loudly.

WRONG: You could have behaved considerable more scrupulously.

RIGHT: You could have behaved *considerably* more scrupulously.

WRONG: He rolled right up my alley rueful fast.

RIGHT: He rolled right up my alley *ruefully* fast.

*She incorrigibly gave herself over to idle and
lascivious pleasures.*

Adjectives, Adverbs, and Linking Verbs

If the modifier, whether it describes or limits, belongs to the subject and not to the verb, it is an adjective.

> Dafne is *jumpy.* (*Jumpy* modifies the noun, *Dafne.*)
> She looks *anxious.* (*Anxious* modifies *she.*)
> Nemo looks *cunning.* (*Cunning* modifies *Nemo.*)
> The mousse tasted *plush.* (*Plush* modifies *mousse,* not *tasted.*)

If the modifier describes the verb, however, it is an adverb, not an adjective. In such cases, the verb is not a linking verb; it describes the action or state of being of the subject.

> She looks *anxiously* at the creaking door.
> He looks *cunningly* at the floor.

To recapitulate an earlier illumination: copulative, or linking, verbs connect a subject to the subjective complement. See page 29 if you care to know what these erotic verbs are.

> Her lips felt *eager.* (*Eager* is the subjective complement of the verb *felt.*)
> She kissed him *eagerly.* (*Eagerly* is an adverb modifying the verb *kissed.*)
> Her *eager* lips kissed him. (*Eager* is an adjective modifying the noun *lips.*)

> She seems *incorrigible.* (*Incorrigible* is the subjective complement of the verb *seems.*)
> She behaves *incorrigibly.* (*Incorrigibly* is an adverb modifying the verb *behaves.*)

She *incorrigibly* gave herself over to idle and
lascivious pleasures. (*Incorrigibly* is an adverb
modifying the verb *gave*.)

She seems *indifferent*. (*Indifferent* is the subjective
complement of the verb *seems*.)
She wriggled *indifferently*. (*Indifferently* is an
adverb modifying the verb *wriggled*.)
She *indifferently* incurred his wrath. (*Indifferently*
is an adverb modifying the verb *incurred*.)

He grew *choleric*. (*Choleric* is the subjective
complement of the verb *grew*.)
He jeered *cholerically*. (*Cholerically* is an adverb
modifying the verb *jeered*.)

The words *good* and *well, bad* and *badly,* are often mis-
used. *Good* and *bad* are adjectives; *well* and *badly* are
adverbs.

WRONG: He tangoes *bad*.

RIGHT: He tangoes *badly*.

WRONG: This contraption works *good*.

RIGHT: This contraption works *well*.

Comparative and Superlative Forms

Adjectives and adverbs come in three forms: positive
(that is, they simply state an attribute), comparative
(they compare an attribute of two things or actions), and
superlative (they compare an attribute of three or more
things or actions).

ADJECTIVES:

Positive	Comparative	Superlative
bad	worse	worst
good	better	best
glum	glummer	glummest
toothsome	more toothsome	most toothsome
racy	racier	raciest
bleak	bleaker	bleakest
idyllic	more idyllic	most idyllic

WRONG: He is the *cutest* of the two mutants.

RIGHT: He is the *cuter* of the two mutants.

RIGHT: He is the *cutest* mutant I've laid my eyeballs on.

WRONG: It is the *least delicate* of the two conditions.

RIGHT: It is the *less delicate* of the two conditions.

RIGHT: Of all conditions, it is the *least delicate*.

WRONG: She's the *niftier* nymph in the forest.

RIGHT: Of the two nymphs, she's the *niftier*.

RIGHT: She's the *niftiest* nymph he ever squeezed.

Don't commit the redundancy of using *more* with the

comparative form of an adjective. The same goes for *most* with the superlative.

WRONG: His contraption is *more better* than mine.

RIGHT: His contraption is *better* than mine.

WRONG: She's the *most daffiest* dowager that ever guzzled tea.

RIGHT: She's the *daffiest* dowager that ever guzzled tea.

ADVERBS:

Positive	Comparative	Superlative
well	better	best
badly	more badly	most badly
woozily	more woozily	most woozily
solemnly	less solemnly	least solemnly
smugly	more smugly	most smugly
drowsily	more drowsily	most drowsily
uncouthly	less uncouthly	least uncouthly

WRONG: Of the two gargoyles, Esmeralda likes the simian one *best*.

RIGHT: Of the two gargoyles, Esmeralda likes the simian one *better*.

RIGHT: Of all the gargoyles Esmeralda has sampled, she likes the simian one *best*.

His contraption is better than mine.

❋ PRONOUNS ❋

When a pronoun follows its nature and substitutes for a noun, the noun is called the antecedent of the pronoun. Thanks to the existence of pronouns, we are spared a soporific redundancy in literature, speech, and songs. Regard the difference:

> Columbine combed the snarls out of
>   Columbine's hair and scrubbed Columbine's
>   body with the loofa Columbine's paramour
>   had given the paramour's true love.

> Columbine combed the snarls out of her hair and
>   scrubbed her body with the loofa her
>   paramour had given his true love.

There are eight kinds of pronouns—personal, interrogative, indefinite, relative, demonstrative, reciprocal, reflexive, and intensive—and we shall admire them all.

Personal Pronouns

Personal pronouns stand in for a person. Besides number

and case, they are distinguished by person: first, second, or third, depending on whether (1) the person is speaking, (2) the person is being spoken to, or (3) the person is being spoken of. (This applies to things as well. A thing may be mute, but it can be gossiped about.) For example:

> *Nemo* suspected that *Dafne* feared *ghosts.*
> *He* suspected that *she* feared *them.*

Number	Person	Nominative Case	Objective Case	Possessive Case
Singular	1st	I	me	my, mine
	2nd	you	you	your, yours
	3rd	he	him	his
		she	her	her, hers
		it	it	its
Plural	1st	we	us	our, ours
	2nd	you	you	your, yours
	3rd	they	them	their, theirs

She is definitely an entity.

May *I* offer you *my* sympathy?
You may offer *it* but *I* won't take *it.*

We all ended up somewhere with *our* various
uncertain lives flapping about *us* in tatters and
our pockets full of foreign coins.

Coming into a clearing in the forest that did not
show on *their* map, *they* tilted *their* puzzled
heads heavenward to discover a corresponding
tear in the sky.

We all ended up somewhere with our various uncertain lives flapping about us in tatters and our pockets full of foreign coins.

Interrogative Pronouns

Interrogative pronouns pose questions: *who, whom, which, what,* or *whose?* *

> *Who* screeched?
> *Which* is my fiancé?
> *What* happens now?
> *Whom* did I marry?
> *Whose* are these shoes?

Indefinite Pronouns

Indefinite pronouns refer to no one in particular; they are noncommittal but useful nevertheless. The indefinite pronouns are *one, someone, anyone, everyone, no one, nobody, several, each, all, neither, either, both, many, few, any, some,* and others of this same hazy ilk.

> *One* does have one's scruples, after all.
> *Several* went to bed.
> *Few* forgive without a fuss.
> *Nobody* is to be found.
> *Everyone* has disappeared.

Relative Pronouns

A relative pronoun is a pronoun that relates to an antecedent (as *that* in the preceding statement relates to *pronoun*) and simultaneously joins it to a limiting or qualifying clause. The relative pronouns in common use are *who, whose, what, which,* and *that.*

* Don't confuse the interrogative pronoun *whose* with *who's*, the contraction for *who is*.

This is the hoax *that* they perpetrated.
She met a sophist *who* surmised her secret.
He posits hypotheses *which* are hair-raising.
She possesses some curious organs, *which* are
    vestigial.

Who refers only to persons, who may be intelligent living beings.

He adored the debutante *who* was staring into
    space.
I awaited the lummox *who* was rolling right up
    my alley.
The diva, *who* was on the skids, was guzzling
    muscatel.
The barber *who* found the nose in his croissant
    never did get along with his wife.

Which refers only to animals and to inanimate, unmoving things. *That* refers to animals and things, and sometimes to persons.

She tickled his fancy, *which* was in need of a
    good laugh.
The ocelot *that* she lost was wearing a costly fur
    coat.
Ask your crystal ball, *which* is the source and
    satiety of your prejudice.
The note, *which* she mangled in her pocket, lost
    its meaning in this fashion and place.
The chair *that* she chanced to sit in was wearing
    two pairs of boots.
An inamorata *that* oscillates can be exasperating.

What is an indefinite relative pronoun, which means that

Few forgive without a fuss.

it stands in for an antecedent that has not been defined. It works like this:

> Take *what* you want.
> Filch *what* you wish.
> Covet *what* you crave.
> Jabber *what* you think.

To express a possessive relative pronoun, use either *whose* or the forms *of whom* or *of which*.

> The werewolf, *whose* fang I told you about, is in unbearable pain.
> The werewolf, the wife *of whom* I mentioned, sobbed relentlessly.
> We like werewolves *whose* teeth are in tip-top shape.
> We like the werewolves, the teeth *of whom* must be in tip-top shape.
> They prefer those chairs, the feet *of which* don't shuffle.

Compound relative pronouns are produced by adding *-ever* to *who, whom, what,* or *which*. These pronouns refer to any person or thing, limitlessly.

> Abandon yourself to *whatever* tickles your fancy.
> Nuzzle *whomever* you please.
> Ogle *whoever* pleases you.

Demonstrative Pronouns

Demonstrative pronouns point out. *This, that, these,* and *those* are demonstrative, pointing to whatever you want them to.

This is my life.
Those are your desires.
These are my misgivings.
That is my answer.

Reciprocal Pronouns

Reciprocal pronouns *each other* and *one another* involve an exchange, however trite or bizarre.

> The two maids cleaned *each other*.
> The vampires gossiped with *one another* until the first gleam of morning light made them kiss *one another* good night.
> The fauns were visibly fond of *each other* and polished *each other's* hooves.

Reflexive Pronouns

Reflexive pronouns are pronouns that refer to the self as an object, bouncing back in its own direction to whatever purpose it has in mind.

> He bit *himself*.
> She made a pact with *herself* to never consort with fascists, pimps, or thugs.

Do not use a -*self* pronoun where a personal pronoun belongs.

> WRONG: Ludwig and *myself* wed.
> RIGHT: Ludwig and *I* wed.

It is he who was dragged in by the cat.

WRONG: She tossed a dirty look at Melissa and *myself.*

RIGHT: She tossed a dirty look at Melissa and *me.*

Intensive Pronouns

Intensive pronouns are *-self* pronouns that one drags in for emphasis.

> You *yourself* are the protagonist.
> I *myself* am the soubrette.

The Cases of Pronouns

Like beer, like wine, like whiskey, pronouns come in cases: nominative case, objective case, and possessive case.

Nominative Case

Nominative pronouns are subject pronouns; they include *I, you, he, she, it, we, they, who, what, which,* and many more.

A subject pronoun functions either as the subject of a verb or as a subjective complement (you remember subjective complements, don't you?).

SUBJECT OF A VERB:

> *I* apologize.
> *He* forgives.

Give a morsel of hope to me.

Who complains?
He throbs.
She twitches.
They smooch.
That feels marvelous.
Which of us is hurt?

THE SUBJECTIVE COMPLEMENT always follows some form of *to be*. Pronouns that act as subjective complements are predicate pronouns.

It is *she* who is dressed to kill.
It is *he* who was dragged in by the cat.
It is *I* who have hot pants.

Objective Case

Pronouns in the objective case are called object pronouns. An object pronoun functions as a direct object, an object of a preposition, an indirect object, or the subject of an infinitive. Object pronouns include *me, you, him, her, it, us, them, whom, which, this, that, these,* and *those.*

DIRECT OBJECT:

I kissed *him.*
Whom did I desire?
He clasped *me.*
I ravished *it.*

OBJECT OF A PREPOSITION:

Give a morsel of hope to *me.*
Go sing your succulent syllables to *him.*
Get that trashy trinket for *her.*

INDIRECT OBJECT:

> Don't tell *me* you've been out with the boys!
> Don't give *me* any more of your lip.
> She gave *him* the cold shoulder because they had
>   a marmoreal love.
> He gave *her* a recording of Mahler's *Tenth*
>   because he was not quite finished with her.

SUBJECT OF AN INFINITIVE:

> She wanted *him* to slumber in her wake.
> He wished *her* to tuck him in first.

Possessive Case

The possessive case is used to denote ownership or to attribute a quality or characteristic to someone or something. A pronoun in the possessive case may stand in for that someone or something, as the following examples of possessive personal pronouns demonstrate:

> *My* thoughts are guarded by indiscretion.
> Thank you for *your* inscrutable honesty.
> It took the prince a while to find *her* lips.
> We put *our* best feet forward and crushed each
>   other's toes.
> *Their* samovar was stolen, and all *their* left socks
>   and shoes.

To form the possessive case of an indefinite pronoun, just add an apostrophe and an *s* to the pronoun.

> *someone's* misfortune
> *anyone's* boo-boo
> *everyone's* fault

For personal pronouns, there is *no* apostrophe in the possessive case.

> The Weltschmerz is *his*.
> The ennui is *hers*.

The relative or interrogative pronoun in the possessive case is quite complete without an apostrophe.

> *Whose* is this libretto?
> The maestro, *whose* lips were quivering, was
>   about to make himself scarce.

Possessive pronouns are often used with gerunds (see page 41):

> We admired *her* curtseying.
> She resented *our* clapping.

Deciding Which Case Is Which

The case of a relative pronoun depends upon its use in a sentence, and it's up to you to figure it out.

> Frisk *whoever* enters.

(*Whoever*, in the nominative case, is the subject of the verb *enters* in the clause *whoever enters*, which acts as the direct object of the verb *frisk*.)

> Fondle *whomever* you wish.

(*Whomever*, in the objective case, is the indirect object of the verb *wish* in the clause *whomever you wish*, which acts as the direct object of the verb *fondle*.)

> Show the door to *whoever* resists.

(*Whoever resists* is a noun clause acting as the object of the

Let's you and me get together and do away with some of the possibilities.

preposition *to*. *Whoever* is the subject of the verb *resists* and therefore must be in the nominative case. See the chapter on clauses for help.)

A pronoun in apposition to a noun or another pronoun has the same case as the word it identifies.

> Two misfits, *he* and *she*, plighted their troth in this haphazard way.
>
> Let's *you* and *me* get together and do away with some of the possibilities.

(*You* and *me* are in apposition with *'s*, which equals *us*, the object of *let*.)

⧉ ARRIVING AT ⧉ AGREEMENTS

One of the ways in which a grammatical relationship is revealed in a sentence is by agreement, that is, using the correct forms of verbs with their subjects and the correct pronouns with their antecedents. There are some specific circumstances in which special attention to agreement must be paid. A verb, for instance, must agree with its subject in number, in spite of any internal distractions obscuring just what that number is. Using the correct verb form helps clarify one's meaning. A pronoun, too, must reflect the number of its antecedent: *they* does not refer to one person, no matter how many personalities *he has*.

Intervening words between subject and verb should not distract from the meaning of the sentence. Even with the presence of a phrase (see the chapter on phrases) mucking up the middle ground between them, a subject and verb must agree.

> An *entourage* of hangers-on *was* sprawling in the lounge.

A *coven* of baby witches and warlocks *was* spotted on the moor.

The number of the subject is not altered by parenthetical expressions introduced by words such as *with, like, together with, as well as, including,* or *no less than.*

> *Weltschmerz,* in addition to ennui, *gives* our courtship a real flair.
>
> *Rosie,* together with the cabbie, *is* rounding the corner in a cab.
>
> The *moppets,* as well as their chaperone, *have* tendered their thanks to the host.

Two or more subjects joined by *and* can't make it through a sentence on anything less than a plural verb.

> An aficionado and a cretin *are* sharing a pitcher of beer.
>
> *Are* the sandman and the vampire buddies?

There are some exceptions, however, to this wavering rule. If the two subjects refer to the same person or thing, the verb is singular.

> My sidekick and bête noire *has* arrived.

(*Sidekick* and *bête noire* identify the same difficult companion.)

Another exception turns up when *each* or *every* precedes singular subjects joined by *and;* then again a singular verb will do the trick.

> Each huzza and hallelujah *was* bouncing off the dome.
>
> Every truncheon and hatchet *was* safely in its place.

My sidekick and bête noire has arrived.

Two or more singular subjects joined by *or* or *nor* waltz to the same singular verb.

> Lucy or Ludwig *is* going to make a mistake.

When singular and plural subjects are joined by *either . . . or, neither . . . nor, not only . . . but also, not . . . but*, or *but not*, the verb must agree with the subject nearest to it:

> Neither Kitsch nor its *proponents were* ridiculed out of the show.
> Not only the patrons, but also the *curator was* unduly cruel.
> Not the vampires but the *sandman has* made a mess of this schloss.
> All the gargoyles but not a single *man was* obliging to her.
> Not the maestro but his *sycophants have* decided to blow this joint.

It is with its subject that a verb agrees, not with its subjective complement.

> His pantaloons *are* a problem for the king.
> The king's problem *is* his pantaloons.

> Her hankerings *are* her downfall.
> Her downfall *is* her hankerings.

> Vertices *are* the ecstasy of triangles.
> The ecstasy of triangles *is* vertices.

Nouns that are plural in form but are singular in meaning take singular verbs. Common nouns of this type include *physics, mathematics, ethics, checkers, measles, mumps, molasses, economics, politics,* and *statistics.*

> Ethics *is* her toughest subject.

Mumps *is* deforming the vampires.

Politics *is* the passion of the very cruel and the
very just.

The molasses that pours into her wheedling *slows*
down when she is crossed.

Some nouns in plural form but with singular intentions
may take plural verbs. Among these mavericks we find
scissors, pliers, tweezers, and *trousers* worn by anyone.

The pliers *were* used to open her mouth, which
was refusing to speak.

The scissors had made a mess of the heavens'
geometry, and *were* preparing to swoop down
on Earth.

Her trousers *were* held up by a pair of suspenders
that clutched her waist with tiny hands.

Singular pronouns take singular verbs. Singular pronouns
include *each, either, neither, everybody, everyone, anybody,
anyone, somebody, someone, nobody,* and *no one.*

Everyone is waltzing to a different Johann Strauss.

Neither of them *was* eager for the contretemps to
end.

Either of the possibilities to lunch on *is* bound to
be a mistake.

Neither of the juggernauts *is* on my list of
Absolutes.

Any, all, such, and *none* may be singular or plural, depending on the intended meaning.

Have any of you made up your spluttering
minds?

Are all of us going to be punished?

Neither of them was eager for the contretemps to end.

Is all the cake devoured?

Collective nouns should be accompanied by singular verbs when the collection is to be taken as a unit.

> The *horde is* gathering and cavorting on the shore.
> The *cult is* growing too big for the britches of Swami Sham.

Collective nouns take plural verbs when the group is meant to be thought of as individuals.

> The *committee were* shuffling their feet and scratching their many heads.
> As the fire blazed the *octet were* rushed to the open door, but they couldn't escape.

A literary title takes a singular verb, even if it contains a plural subject.

> "Tidings from Timofey," a Slavic ghost story, concerns a specter who is afraid of the dark.
> *Colloquies Among the Sybarites* is a smashing new Off Broadway hit.
> "Fear and Trembling in the Aquarium" is a cantata about angst in the lower forms of life.

In sentences that begin with the expletive *there* (as in *there is, there are, there exists, there exist*), the subject follows the verb and is the critical factor in choosing a singular or plural verb form; *there* is not the subject, nor will it ever be.

> WRONG: There *exists* many beasts in the wilderness that I'd rather not discuss.

> RIGHT: There *exist* many beasts in the wilderness that I'd rather not discuss.

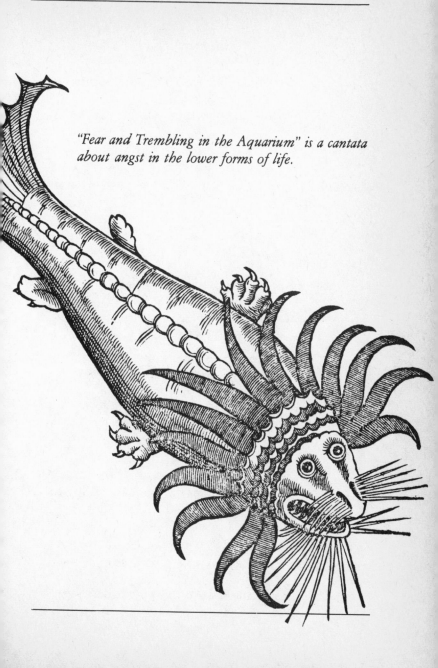

"Fear and Trembling in the Aquarium" is a cantata about angst in the lower forms of life.

There *is* one lonely mummy in the tomb.
There *are* cronies one is better off without.
There *is* a faun in the forest who looks like Blaise Cendrars.
There *are* wraiths among the pachyderms who prefer to go unnamed.

The word *there* may also be used as an adverb, meaning "in that place."

There she sobbed.
There he placed his paw.

The expletive *it* is always followed by a singular verb.

It *is* the little maestro and his hangers-on.
It *was* the vampires who paid a visit to the schloss.
It *is* that ingenue who has such panache.

When taken as a unit (and money's always taken gladly by someone), sums of money and measurements require a singular verb.

Five hundred bucks *is* her bottom line.
Twenty years *is* the maximum I am willing to suffer this ruckus with you.

When not intended to be thought of as a unit, sums of money and measurements take a plural verb.

The five hundred dollars *were* well thumbed.

The twenty years you inflicted on me *were* the
    juiciest years of my life.

Whether relative pronouns (*who, which, that, what*) are
singular or plural depends on their antecedents, which in
this case call the shots.

He is the only mutant *who knows* how to sing the
    blues.
He is one of many mutants *who hang* around this
    dive.
They *who are* leap-frogging on the front lawn are
    in for a big surprise.
It is I *who am* the culprit in "The Case of the
    Missing Gorgonzola."

A pronoun should agree with its antecedent in number.
Singular pronouns should be used to refer to antecedents
such as *person, man, woman, someone, somebody, anyone, anybody, either, neither, each, everyone,* and *everybody.*

Everyone scratched *his* forearm and took another
    drag.
Each of the supplicants was given *his* own
    licorice whip.

Even when a subject comes hot on the heels of its verb, it
is still the verb that must agree in number with the
subject.

Gawking out of the corner of his eye *was* a *man*
    who adored stevedores.
Beneath the honeysuckle *were* the *caresses* he had
    longed for being given to another man.
Out of the mouth of the little maestro *issues* a
    monologue from "Waiting for Godot."

Two or more antecedents joined by *and* take a plural pronoun.

> Samson and Delilah licked *their* chops.
> Rosie and Nimrod rubbed *their* flanks.

Singular antecedents joined by *or* or *nor* take a pronoun that's singular, too.

> Neither Nimbus nor Quercus will present *his* rosebud to the queen.

In reference to one singular and one plural antecedent, the pronoun agrees with the nearer antecedent.

> Neither abduction nor nuptials had *their* place on the agenda for tonight.
> Neither nuptials nor abduction had *its* place on the agenda for tonight.

Collective nouns may take a singular or plural pronoun, depending on their meanings.

> The entourage is abandoning *its* turf and is walking out in a huff. (It was moving as a unit.)
> The entourage lolling about in the lobby were hanging out *their* tongues. (Apparently this was an existential act for each of them.)
> The Styrian String Quartet is a four-headed monster of catgut and mediocrity that shouldn't be let out of *its* cage.

Demonstrative pronouns (*this, that, these, those*) should agree with the nouns they modify.

The entourage lolling about in the lobby were hanging out their tongues.

She has a propensity for that sort of muddle.

WRONG: She has a propensity for *those* sort of muddles.

RIGHT: She has a propensity for *that* sort of muddle.

RIGHT: She has a propensity for *those* sorts of muddles.

WRONG: He pursues *those* kind of nymphs.

RIGHT: He pursues *that* kind of nymph.

RIGHT: He pursues *those* kinds of nymphs.

✦ PHRASES ✦

Among the many delightful things you might find in a sentence is a phrase. A phrase is a group of words (in succession) from which both subject and verb are absent.* A phrase has many interesting possibilities nevertheless: it may be used as a noun, adjective, adverb, or verb.

Prepositional Phrases

A prepositional phrase is composed of a preposition plus an object of the preposition and its modifiers. The prepositional phrase may act as an adjective, adverb, or noun.

ADJECTIVE:

> The nude *in the next room* slid off the wall.
> The damsel *with the bedroom eyes* is my grandma.
> Her mug, *with its inscrutable torpor,* is
> enthralling.

---

* A phrase may contain a clause within it that *does* contain a subject and a verb.

*To nuzzle flagpoles is her
secret desire.*

ADVERB:

> The proselytizer hopped *over the threshold.*
> The housecoated heathen hissed raffishly *through her teeth.*

NOUN:

> *Out of my depth* is where I'm likely to be.
> *Beyond the pale* is the penultimate stop of this train.
> *Beneath the bridge* is the spot where she took her cares.

Infinitive Phrases

An infinitive phrase is what you get by combining an infinitive with an object. It may be used as a noun, adjective, or adverb.

NOUN:

> *To nuzzle flagpoles* is her secret desire. (subject)
> She longs *to nuzzle flagpoles.* (direct object)
> Her secret hankering is *to nuzzle flagpoles.*
>   (subjective complement)
> She has no hankering except *to nuzzle flagpoles.*
>   (object of preposition *except*)

ADJECTIVE:

> I have a suggestion *to thrust upon you.* (modifies *suggestion*)
> She conjured up visions of unearthly buffoons *to while away her dread.* (modifies *visions*)

He had a mood *to suit every occasion*. (modifies *mood*)

ADVERB:

He simpered *to mollify her*. (modifies *simpered*)
He was uncouth *to impress her*. (modifies *uncouth*)
She was startled *to like him*. (modifies *startled*)

Participial Phrases

The participial phrase begins with either a present or a past participle and is used as an adjective.

PRESENT PARTICIPLE:

The genius *lounging on the lawn* is my nemesis.
The grimace *dancing on her lips* slithered into a smirk.
The ghost *leaning against the parapet* decided to sally forth.
The flasher *loafing along the sidelines* was seized with a fit of pudeur.
The physicist *shambling provocatively up to the lectern* was a case of $E = mc^2$.

PAST PARTICIPLE:

The rabbit *ejected from the top hat* was a fake.
The starlet, *intoxicated by their cozy chat*, lit a cigar.
The bedroom, *suffused with a slovenly glow*, awaited our belated tryst.
The cul-de-sac *encountered at the end of the road* contained a secret door.

Gerund Phrases

The gerund phrase is used as a noun, and that's the only way it will ever consent to find itself in a sentence you write. It may function in any way a noun does.

> *Ogling stevedores* is his penchant. (subject)
> He relishes *ogling stevedores*. (direct object)
> His proclivity is *ogling stevedores*. (subjective complement)
> He indulges in *ogling stevedores*. (object of preposition *in*)

Verb Phrases

The verb phrase is made up of the verb and its accomplices, or auxiliaries. The presence of the verb makes the verb phrase different from other phrases, but there is no subject to go with it within the phrase.

> She *has been persuaded* to repent.
> He *is being forced* to recant.
> We *have been invited* to watch.

Absolute Phrases

A combination of a noun or pronoun and a participle results in an absolute phrase. Unlike other phrases, it is grammatically independent of the rest of the sentence, as the situations that follow show.

> *The wine having been poisoned,* he convulsed.

The rabbit ejected from the top hat was a fake.

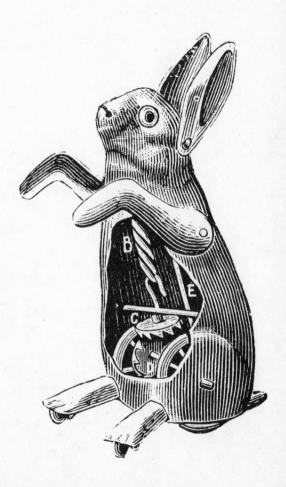

The truth having slipped out, she winked.
Dawn having cracked, the vampire snoozed.
The night being eerie, we quivered.
The baguette plundered, they starved.

❧ CLAUSES ❧

A clause is a group of words containing a subject and predicate. Clauses come in two attitudes: independent and dependent.

Independent Clauses

An independent clause makes sense by itself and could be written as a separate sentence; the term, however, is usually applied to such groups of words when they occur as part of longer sentences.

> I fondled his lapel.
> I fondled his lapel, and I caressed his socks.

(The independent clause *I fondled his lapel* stands alone in the first example and is joined by another independent clause, *I caressed his socks,* in the second.)

> I ruffled his hair, and I beseeched him to relent.
> She was kicked by the soft shoe of destiny, and she landed in Wales.

> The tycoon snapped his avuncular suspenders,
>   and he called for another round.
>
> Her irony is getting rusty, and her audience is
>   bored.
>
> He lifted her comatose toe in his palm, and he
>   pronounced her over the scourge.

Dependent Clauses

A dependent clause is incapable of standing on its own
two feet (even though they are a subject and a verb) and
therefore depends on some other part of the sentence. It is
not that the dependent clause is lacking in the compo-
nents of an independent clause; it is reduced to this abject
condition by the subordinate conjunction that introduces
it.

> I fondled his lapel before I caressed his socks.
>
> If she capitulates, we will reward her with a
>   lollipop.
>
> If this is love, I've made a terrible mistake.
>
> If you'll let out the cat, I'll let out the last word.

Dependent clauses are classified by their use—there are
adjective clauses and adverb clauses—and these classifications are further classified.

Adjective Clauses

An adjective clause modifies a noun or pronoun.

> The dowager *who struck the match* was a
>   pyromaniac.
>
> The hedonist *who was looking at his watch* began
>   to scratch his crotch.

If this is love, I've made a terrible mistake.

Everyone *who had a gripe* was gagged and bound
at the door.

The Lilliputian *who was dressed in yellow silk* sang
to her flea in its cage.

That beard, *which sits so awkwardly upon his face,*
looks like a toupee for the chin.

Adjective clauses can be restrictive or nonrestrictive. A
restrictive clause imparts information needed to identify
the person or thing it is modifying.

The girl *who is stroking the gargoyle* is in love.

(The adjective clause tells *which* girl is in love.)

A nonrestrictive clause gives descriptive information not
strictly essential to the sentence.

Esmeralda Waterloo, *who strokes gargoyles,* is in
love.

(Although the information in the clause may be interesting, it is not strictly necessary for identifying this per-
vert, whose name is given.)

If an adjective clause can be left out without altering the
meaning of the sentence, it is nonrestrictive. If the clause
is essential to the meaning, it is restrictive.

The specter *that is lurching down the street* is my
pal. (restrictive)

The hand *that is languishing on the windowsill*
once was mine. (restrictive)

The marks *that are fading on my throat* are not
fresh. (restrictive)

The hand that is languishing on the windowsill
once was mine.

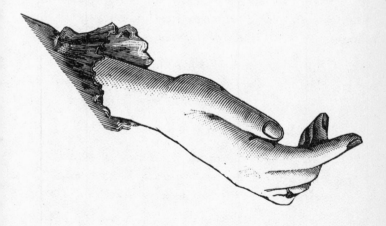

The specter, *which lurched its way beyond my sight,* gave out a piercing shriek. (nonrestrictive)

The languishing hand, *which once was mine,* applauded. (nonrestrictive)

The marks, *which are not fresh,* were caused by neither beast nor man. (nonrestrictive)

Esmeralda Waterloo, *who is in love,* strokes gargoyles. (nonrestrictive)

Only a person *who loves gargoyles* can love human beings. (restrictive)

Orpheus, *who showed up in a zoot suit,* wailed on his saxophone. (nonrestrictive)

Adverb Clauses

An adverb clause behaves in the same manner as a one-word adverb. An adverb clause that indicates time is introduced by such words as *before, after, until,* or *when.*

I'll bring you back *before I take you away.*

She ran away from the commune *when she was assigned to clean out the ears.*

An adverb clause can point to a place.

We sought the truth *where it was least obvious.*

He followed her *wherever she ambled or rolled.*

He scratched her flesh *where he imagined it itched.*

An adverb clause that expresses manner starts out with *as* or *as if.*

He bounced along in his checked suit *as if the world were his.*

An adverb clause can indicate cause.

> I laughed *because I was miffed.*
> I scowled, *since I was thrilled.*
> He left *because he was perplexed.*
> We made up, *since we were inseparable.*

An adverb clause stating a condition is introduced by such terms as *if, unless,* and *provided that.*

> *If you spank me,* I will comply.
> *Unless I am mistaken,* we've already been through that.

An adverb clause can indicate purpose.

> She shuddered *in order that she might find relief.*
> He whispered softly *so that she would draw nearer the fire.*
> She took his comfort *that she might save it for later.*

An adverb clause stating a concession starts out with *although, even though,* or *though.*

> He excoriated her behavior *even though he secretly approved.*
> She swooned *though there was a curious gleam in her eye.*
> She stepped into the empty elevator *although she'd already gone as far as she could.*

An adverb clause indicating result is introduced by *that* or *so.*

> He waxed so eloquent *that he made his point too soon.*
> We were enfeebled by his cajolery, *so we left.*

An adverb clause can show comparison.

She has strayed farther than most lost sheep.

Her billowing voice is as voluminous *as a résumé of the wind.* (It is understood that *as a résumé of the wind is* is meant.)

She has strayed farther *than most lost sheep* [*have strayed*].

Her gullibility is more remarkable *than her sins* [*are*].

Noun Clauses

A noun clause saunters about in the same way that a noun or pronoun does.

That she is definitely an entity is a hypothesis he would like to entertain. (subject)

He suspects *that she is definitely an entity.* (direct object)

His most unflagging supposition is *that she is definitely an entity.* (subjective complement)

He will take her for *whoever she can prove she is.* (object of preposition *for*)

Sentences Caused by Clauses

Sentences can be classified, if that's what you want to do with them, by the number and kind of clauses they contain. Every grammatically complete sentence has at least one independent clause. The four kinds of sentences are the simple sentence, the compound sentence, the complex sentence, and the compound-complex sentence.

The simple sentence contains one independent clause.

The lithium worked.

The compound sentence has two or more independent clauses.

> The lithium worked, and the mania subsided.
> The lithium worked, the mania subsided, and
> the depression lifted.

The complex sentence has one independent clause and one or more dependent clauses.

> As the lithium took effect, the mania subsided.

The compound-complex sentence is a compound sentence plus one or more dependent clauses.

> As the lithium took effect, the mania subsided
> and the depression lifted.

☙ FRAGMENTS ❧

The sentence fragment, an incomplete sentence punctu-
ated as a sentence, is a grammatical blunder of the most
atrocious order. Trying to pass off a group of words like a
phrase or a subordinate clause as a complete sentence is a
scurrilous mechanical misdeed. A fragment should be
joined to a main clause or rewritten to become a complete
sentence by itself. Even if it contains a subject and predicate, a statement preceded by a subordinate conjunction
will still not make it as a sentence. Watch your step,
buddy.

FRAGMENT: A shade of green which caught her
            eye.

SENTENCE: A shade of green caught her eye.

FRAGMENT: Sometimes bras and panties would
            cry out to her to touch them.
            Navigating her way through the
            boutique.

SENTENCE: Sometimes bras and panties would cry out to her to touch them as she navigated her way through the boutique.

FRAGMENT: The vampire scratched his head thoughtfully. As he bent over his conundrum.

SENTENCE: The vampire scratched his head thoughtfully as he bent over his conundrum.

FRAGMENT: I want more. Because I'm one of those insatiable robots, you know.

SENTENCE: I want more because I'm one of those insatiable robots, you know.

FRAGMENT: Tripping over the ripped linoleum. She was floored.

SENTENCE: Tripping over the ripped linoleum, she was floored.

FRAGMENT: Vague tremors disturbed the room. Which were small and were caused by the electrical storm in the curtains.

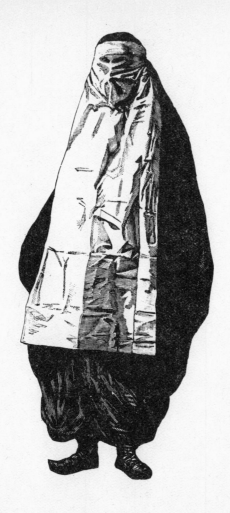

Sometimes bras and panties would cry out to her to touch them as she navigated her way through the boutique.

SENTENCE: The vague tremors disturbing the room were small and were caused by the electrical storm in the curtains.

✹ COMMA SPLICES ✹

Equal in grammatical horror to the sentence fragment is the comma splice. A comma splice results when a comma is placed between two independent clauses without the necessary link of a coordinating conjunction. Most often some other word, like *this, another, there,* or *it,* begins the second clause in an attempt to be the second half of an implausible sentence. Instead of a comma, a period or a semicolon should be used to separate independent clauses.

> SPLICE: One type of protagonist is looking for himself at the bottom of every river, another type is looking for love.

> RIGHT: One type of protagonist is looking for himself at the bottom of every river; another type is looking for love.

> SPLICE: This contraption is most nefarious when set into motion by a velvet-

gloved paw, this combination is a sure killer for the unsuspecting, the naive, and the young at heart.

RIGHT: This contraption is most nefarious when set into motion by a velvet-gloved paw. This combination is a sure killer for the unsuspecting, the naive, and the young at heart.

SPLICE: They had a fatal attraction, it was based on *The Myth of Sisyphus* and a love of Harpo Marx.

RIGHT: They had a fatal attraction; it was based on *The Myth of Sisyphus* and a love of Harpo Marx.

SPLICE: One way to find a sweetheart is to put an ad in the paper, another is to wait and see what the cat drags in.

RIGHT: One way to find a sweetheart is to put an ad in the paper; another is to wait and see what the cat drags in.

SPLICE: She wrapped herself up in an enigma, there was no other way to keep warm.

RIGHT: She wrapped herself up in an enigma; there was no other way to keep warm.

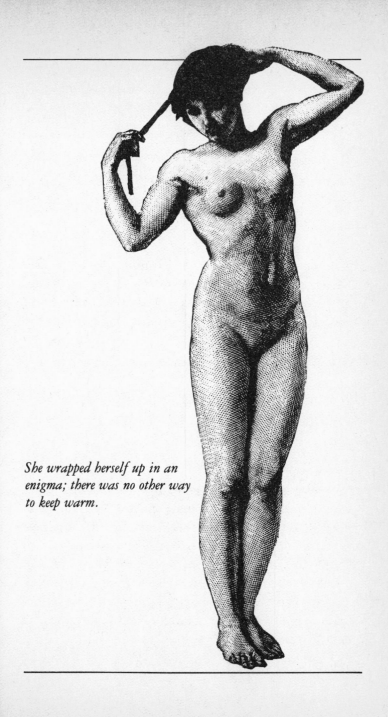

She wrapped herself up in an enigma; there was no other way to keep warm.

SPLICE: Little fauns are stroked on their haunches when they become too raucous, this calms their frisky young nerves.

RIGHT: Little fauns are stroked on their haunches when they become too raucous. This calms their frisky young nerves.

There are instances in which a comma should be used instead of a semicolon. When the clauses are concise and similar in construction or when the sentence has a casual lilt, use a comma between the clauses.

I could hardly believe my senses, he so relieved my fever.
She darkened his door, he lit her fire, they both burned.
Have gun, will travel.

Two independent clauses joined by a conjunctive adverb can also hurl you into a comma splice. The conjunctive adverbs to watch out for in this particular little minefield are: *accordingly, afterwards, also, besides, consequently, earlier, hence, however, later, moreover, nevertheless, otherwise, still, then, therefore,* and *thus*. These words express relationships between two clauses or sentences, such as condition, time, contrast, accumulation, and cause and effect. Tread carefully.

SPLICE: The intruders never failed to arrive with bonbons and champagne, hence they were always welcome at the schloss.

RIGHT: The intruders never failed to arrive with bonbons and champagne. Hence, they were always welcome at the schloss.

SPLICE: The grandee bought himself a pair of roller skates, accordingly he rolled down the avenida in his shirt-sleeves with an unsteadiness unbecoming to his rank.

RIGHT: The grandee bought himself a pair of roller skates. Accordingly, he rolled down the avenida in his shirt-sleeves with an unsteadiness unbecoming to his rank.

SPLICE: The angels are dancing the saraband on the head of a pin, afterwards they'll cool their heels in the River Styx.

RIGHT: The angels are dancing the saraband on the head of a pin. Afterwards they'll cool their heels in the River Styx.

SPLICE: Her attention was diverted by a movement in the curtains, otherwise she only had eyes for him.

RIGHT: Her attention was diverted by a movement in the curtains; otherwise she only had eyes for him.

▓ THE CREATION ▓ OF SENTENCES

Emphasis, unity, and coherence make a sentence effective and make its meaning clear. Although short sentences can have a strong effect when used sparingly, in the right instance, they can give a choppy, simple-minded impression if used in rapid succession, too often, or carelessly. Short, blunt sentences can be combined in a number of ways to expand on their meaning by creating or revealing relationships or by conveying new rhythms. Rhythm is as important a part of a well-written sentence as grammatical correctness. Notice how short and simple sentences can be changed in the following suggested variations.

Yolanta became tipsy. She felt a rage for life. It was surging. An attractive new trauma caused this. She was yanked out of her tedium.

Yanked out of her tedium by an attractive new trauma, Yolanta became tipsy with a surging rage for life.

An attractive new trauma yanking her out of her
tedium, Yolanta became tipsy with a surging
rage for life.

Surging with a rage for life, Yolanta was yanked
out of her tedium by an attractive new
trauma.

He was sadistic. His particular specialty was
contumely. Melissa craved it. She was thirsty
for it. This thirst was abject.

His particular sadistic specialty was contumely,
which Melissa craved with an abject thirst.

The travelers rubbed their eyes. They were
weary. They couldn't believe them. It was so
trite. It was a mirage. The mirage was made
of clouds, a stream of gold, some fabulous
animals, and some old shoes.

Unable to believe their eyes, the weary travelers
rubbed them, for the mirage, made of clouds,
a stream of gold, some fabulous animals, and
some old shoes, was so trite.

The weary travelers rubbed their disbelieving
eyes at the sight of the trite mirage, which
was made of clouds, a stream of gold, some
fabulous animals, and old shoes.

The impostor gloated. The last piece of his little
game was in place. It had fallen there deftly.
His eyes glimmered slyly.

*His particular sadistic specialty was contumely, which
Melissa craved with an abject thirst.*

His eyes glimmering slyly, the impostor gloated over the last piece of his little game, which had fallen deftly into place.

The last piece of his little game having fallen deftly into place, the impostor gloated with slyly glimmering eyes.

The megalomaniac was scudding. He crossed the vestibule. His harem was waiting for him. They were in an uproar.

His harem awaiting him in an uproar, the megalomaniac scudded across the vestibule.

In an uproar, the harem awaited the megalomaniac scudding across the vestibule.

Scudding across the vestibule, the megalomaniac was awaited by his uproarious harem.

He had made her acquaintance. It was amiable. She was a purveyor of ambrosias. She was lying asprawl. She was on a divan. It was a divan of a curious Persian design.

He had made the amiable acquaintance of a purveyor of ambrosias who was lying asprawl a divan of a curious Persian design.

The ravine gaped. The heat was merciless. The bandits pursued their course. It was insidious.

In the merciless heat, the bandits pursued their insidious course through the gaping ravine.

Though the heat was merciless and the ravine gaping, the bandits pursued their insidious course.

Insidiously pursuing their course through the merciless heat, the bandits traversed the gaping ravine.

Through the mercilessly hot and gaping ravine, the bandits pursued their insidious course.

The bandits, pursuing their insidious course through the merciless heat, were swallowed by the gaping ravine.

She was lying. She was dreaming. Her dreams were of biceps and divorce. She was in her rickety garret. It was crawling with rats.

In her rickety garret, which was crawling with rats, she lay dreaming of biceps and divorce.

Dreaming of biceps and divorce, she lay in her rickety garret, which was crawling with rats.

Dreaming of biceps and divorce, she lay in her rickety, rat-infested garret.

Dreaming of biceps and divorce, she crawled about her rickety garret with the rats.

The train clacked along. The conductor was thumbing a girlie magazine. He was singing "Makin' Whoopee." He was cockeyed.

As the train clacked along, the cockeyed
conductor thumbed a girlie magazine and
sang "Makin' Whoopee."

Thumbing a girlie magazine and singing
"Makin' Whoopee," the cockeyed conductor
clacked along in the train.

Cockeyed, the conductor thumbed a girlie
magazine and sang "Makin' Whoopee" in the
clacking-along train.

One thumb in a girlie magazine and "Makin'
Whoopee" on his lips, the cockeyed
conductor distracted himself as the train
clacked along.

In creating sentences, in projecting your thoughts onto
paper, in your tortured efforts to communicate, you
would be well advised to follow the following injunc-
tions, exhortations, intimations against possible lurking
blunders which I hope to spare you from making by noti-
fying you of them at once.

Double Negatives

A double negative is what you end up with (and what
your reader is insulted or puzzled by) if you combine two
words that express negation (such as *no* and *nothing* or *no*
and *not*) to make a single negative statement. This is un-
acceptable grammatical behavior and you will be brutally
chastised for it, believe me.

*In her rickety garret, which was crawling with rats, she lay
dreaming of biceps and divorce.*

WRONG: It didn't make no sense to the debutante that her life should have started at all.

RIGHT: It didn't make any sense to the debutante that her life should have started at all.

RIGHT: It made no sense to the debutante that her life should have started at all.

WRONG: You don't owe me nothing, but give me something anyway.

RIGHT: You don't owe me anything, but give me something anyway.

RIGHT: You owe me nothing, but give me something anyway.

Since the words *hardly* and *scarcely* and *barely* are negative in meaning, you shouldn't double them up with *not*.

WRONG: I couldn't hardly gild the lily with what was left in my pocket after that.

RIGHT: I could hardly gild the lily with what was left in my pocket after that.

WRONG: He couldn't barely resist her with that lunar Band-Aid of a smirk on her limpid mug.

RIGHT: He could barely resist her with that lunar Band-Aid of a smirk on her limpid mug.

You don't owe me anything,
but give me something
anyway.

WRONG: She couldn't hardly put her best foot forward as long as it was in her mouth.

RIGHT: She could hardly put her best foot forward as long as it was in her mouth.

WRONG: She couldn't scarcely mope in her room in that tawdry get-up and get her comeuppance, too.

RIGHT: She could scarcely mope in her room in that tawdry get-up and get her comeuppance, too.

That

Keep *that* out of the realm of superfluity, where it won't do you any good.

WRONG: We know *that*, although he is patting her midriff, *that* things will go no further for quite some time.

RIGHT: We know *that*, although he is patting her midriff, things will go no further for quite some time.

WRONG: They supposed *that*, even if they melted down all the calendars and smashed all the clocks, *that* one minute would daftly follow another until some final cure were found for the malady of Time.

RIGHT: They supposed *that,* even if they melted down all the calendars and smashed all the clocks, one minute would daftly follow another until some final cure were found for the malady of Time.

Painful Separations

Don't needlessly separate related parts of a sentence, as misplacement of clauses or phrases can seriously distort your meaning. Subject and predicate should not be sundered brutally.

WRONG: You, waiting relentlessly for me at the corner, howled.

RIGHT: Waiting relentlessly for me at the corner, you howled.

RIGHT: At the corner where you awaited me relentlessly, you howled.

Adverbs *want* to be near the words they modify. This is especially tricky with the adverbs *almost, only, scarcely, nearly, hardly, barely,* and *even.*

WRONG: We scarcely were aware of the menace gliding through the corridor.

RIGHT: We were scarcely aware of the menace gliding through the corridor.

WRONG: The baby vampire only has two more teeth to grow and his mouth will be complete.

RIGHT: The baby vampire has only two more teeth to grow and his mouth will be complete.

WRONG: She even had bought a silver negligee with wings sprouting out of the shoulders, and winged slippers to match.

RIGHT: She had even bought a silver negligee with wings sprouting out of the shoulders, and winged slippers to match.

Phrases, too, long to be placed near the words they modify.

WRONG: Let me know if you'll meet me in the quagmire by phone or telegram.

RIGHT: Let me know by phone or telegram if you'll meet me in the quagmire.

WRONG: The debutante was nuzzling the gargoyle in the Dior dress.

RIGHT: The debutante in the Dior dress was nuzzling the gargoyle.

Clauses, too, clamor to be near the words they modify.

WRONG: She bartered her soul with the cloven-hoofed visitant which she had just found.

RIGHT: She bartered her soul, which she had

just found, with the cloven-hoofed
visitant.

WRONG: He whipped out the ace and flashed
it at his captors that he had up his
sleeve.

RIGHT: He whipped out the ace that he had up
his sleeve and flashed it at his captors.

WRONG: She flung her life beneath an
oncoming train which she had
decided to take.

RIGHT: She flung her life, which she had
decided to take, beneath an oncoming
train.

Avoid what are called "squinting modifiers." A squinting
modifier is one placed between two words so that it could
be construed to modify either word.

SQUINTING: She said yesterday she lost her
ocelot.

CLEAR: Yesterday she said she lost her ocelot.

CLEAR: She said she lost her ocelot yesterday.

SQUINTING: The Doppelgänger who was
grimacing ruthlessly stalked his
other half.

CLEAR: The Doppelgänger who was ruthlessly
grimacing stalked his other half.

CLEAR: The Doppelgänger who was grimacing stalked his other half ruthlessly.

SQUINTING: He says today he'll be right up my alley.

CLEAR: He says he'll be right up my alley today.

CLEAR: Today he says he'll be right up my alley.

Don't split your infinitives. They'd rather remain intact.

WRONG: He begged her *to* indecently *think* of him.

RIGHT: He begged her *to think* indecently of him.

RIGHT: He begged her *to think* of him indecently.

WRONG: She asked him *to* dexterously *manipulate* her.

RIGHT: She asked him *to manipulate* her dexterously.

Dangling Modifiers

Don't leave them hanging around like that!

He begged her to think indecently of him.

DANGLING PARTICIPIAL PHRASES:

WRONG: Rearranging her coiffure, the nocturnal void gaped before her.

RIGHT: Rearranging her coiffure, she contemplated the nocturnal void gaping before her. (She, not the nocturnal void, is rearranging her coiffure.)

WRONG: Scampering away together into a lurid beam of light, a hysterical elation could be felt.

RIGHT: Scampering away together into a lurid beam of light, they could feel a hysterical elation.

RIGHT: Scampering away together into a lurid beam of light, they were hysterically elated.

WRONG: Abandoning all diffidence, a soothing destiny could be sidled up to and be given no more thought.

RIGHT: Abandoning all diffidence, she could sidle up to a soothing destiny without giving it any more thought.

DANGLING GERUND PHRASES:

WRONG: Before pasting his photograph into her Bestiary, a telegram was handed to her.

RIGHT: Before pasting his photograph into her Bestiary, she was handed a telegram.

RIGHT: Before pasting his photograph into her Bestiary, she received a telegram.

WRONG: While dreaming of baboons and periwinkles, her slumbers were interrupted by a hand poised on her throat.

RIGHT: While dreaming of baboons and periwinkles, she was interrupted from her slumbers by a hand poised on her throat.

DANGLING INFINITIVE PHRASES:

WRONG: To be ultimately satisfying, you should arrange your tryst to coincide with several other transgressions as well.

RIGHT: To be ultimately satisfying, a tryst should be arranged to coincide with several other transgressions as well.

RIGHT: To be ultimately satisfying, a tryst should coincide with several other transgressions as well.

DANGLING ELLIPTICAL CLAUSES:

(In an elliptical clause, one or more missing words are understood. In the first example we understand that it was she who was but a little wraith.)

WRONG: While but a little wraith of a sorceress, a hoary old alchemist taught her many spells and curses she was to boggle later in life.

RIGHT: While but a little wraith of a sorceress, she was taught by a hoary old alchemist many spells and curses she was to boggle later in life.

WRONG: When a cherub of four years old, her uncle would put things in his pipe and smoke them as she bounced upon his knee.

RIGHT: When she was a cherub of four years old, her uncle would put things in his pipe and smoke them as she bounced upon his knee.

RIGHT: When a cherub of four years old, she would bounce upon her uncle's knee as he put things in his pipe and smoked them.

WRONG: When not yet past the portals of puberty, her podiatrist pounced on her.

RIGHT: When not yet past the portals of puberty, she was pounced on by her podiatrist.

To be ultimately satisfying, a tryst should coincide with several other transgressions as well.

WRONG: Although holding forth glibly, his
         audience was smothered in ennui.

RIGHT: Although holding forth glibly, he was
         smothering his audience in ennui.

RIGHT: Although he was holding forth glibly,
         his audience was smothered in ennui.

Parallel Structures

To get across ideas of equal value (not as one gets across a
desert, though it may sometimes feel like that), use a
parallel structure, or a structure as parallel as the occasion
demands.

WRONG: She is unfathomable, with a head of
         strawberry blond hair, and has a
         deductive manner.

RIGHT: She is deductive, strawberry blond,
         and unfathomable.

RIGHT: She is an unfathomable, deductive
         strawberry blond.

RIGHT: She is an unfathomable, strawberry
         blond deductress.

WRONG: He is cute, with a pin-striped soul,
         and has a dashing way about him.

RIGHT: He is cute and dashing, with his pin-
         striped soul.

RIGHT: He is cute, dashing, and pin-striped.

When you become a streetwalker, you don't write home very much.

WRONG: The faun is shy, with rough hooves,
and behaves in a sylvan fashion.

RIGHT: The faun is shy, rough-hoofed, and
sylvan.

RIGHT: The rough-hoofed faun is shy and
sylvan.

Shifts

Don't go shifting around person and number of the same
noun in different elements of a sentence.

SHIFTS IN PERSON:

WRONG: When you are in love, one is
oblivious to one's own faults.

RIGHT: When you are in love, you are
oblivious to your own faults.

RIGHT: When one is in love, one is oblivious
to one's own faults.

WRONG: When one becomes a streetwalker,
you don't write home very much.

RIGHT: When one becomes a streetwalker, she
doesn't write home very much.

RIGHT: When you become a streetwalker, you
don't write home very much.

SHIFTS IN NUMBER:

WRONG: If a faun becomes thirsty, they find a
stream.

RIGHT: If a faun becomes thirsty, he finds a stream.

RIGHT: If fauns become thirsty, they find a stream.

WRONG: After a faun takes his nap, they lick their hooves and then rub their eyes.

RIGHT: After a faun takes his nap, he licks his hooves and then rubs his eyes.

RIGHT: After fauns take their naps, they lick their hooves and then rub their eyes.

Furthermore, don't shift your subjects or the voices of your verbs.

SHIFTS IN VOICE:

WRONG: The faun was in love with a nymph named Effie, and many hours were spent each day slinking past her glade.

RIGHT: The faun was in love with a nymph named Effie and spent many hours each day slinking past her glade.

WRONG: The hypotenuse was bored with facing the same old right angle, and its nights were passed in dreams of escape.

RIGHT: The hypotenuse was bored with facing the same old right angle and passed its nights in dreams of escape.

*This story recounts the adventures of a hypochondriac who
has been plagued by an aberrant kneecap and has tried
several miracle cures and then takes matters into his own
hands and drowns himself.*

Verbs may be tense and moody, but don't assume you can shift their tenses and moods whenever the whim seizes you.

SHIFTS IN TENSE:

WRONG: She lumbered across the verandah and proceeds to weep.

RIGHT: She lumbered across the verandah and proceeded to weep.

WRONG: This story recounts the adventures of a hypochondriac who has been plagued by an aberrant kneecap and had tried several miracle cures and then takes matters into his own hands and drowned himself.

RIGHT: This story recounts the adventures of a hypochondriac who has been plagued by an aberrant kneecap and has tried several miracle cures and then takes matters into his own hands and drowns himself.

Keep your commands, advice, and exhortations consistent, instead of staggering around from one mood to another, such as from subjunctive to indicative or from imperative to indicative.

SHIFTS IN MOOD:

WRONG: It is essential that exile circumvent captivity and abounds in obstacles.

RIGHT: It is essential that exile circumvent captivity and abound in obstacles.

WRONG: Flee while there is still time and then you can stop to catch your last breath.

RIGHT: Flee while there is still time and then stop to catch your last breath.

RIGHT: You should flee while there is still time and then you should stop to catch your last breath.

WRONG: Pout coquettishly and then you must ask him wistfully to help you bury the hatchet.

RIGHT: Pout coquettishly and then ask him wistfully to help you bury the hatchet.

RIGHT: You must pout coquettishly and then you must ask him wistfully to help you bury the hatchet.

RIGHT: You must pout coquettishly and then ask him wistfully to help you bury the hatchet.

WRONG: Beckon the transitive vampire to your bedside and then you must submit to his kisses thirstily.

Flee while there is still time and then stop to catch your last breath.

RIGHT: Beckon the transitive vampire to your bedside and submit to his kisses thirstily.

RIGHT: You must beckon the transitive vampire to your bedside and submit to his kisses thirstily.

✶ INDEX ✶